Leatherback Turtle

The World's Heaviest Reptile

by Kirsten Hall

Consultant: Bryan Wallace, Ph.D.
Duke University Center for Marine Conservation
Nicholas School of the Environment and Earth Sciences
Beaufort, NC

BEARPORT
PUBLISHING

New York, New York

Credits

Cover, Herb Segars–www.gotosnapshot.com; 2–3, ©Doug Perrine/Seapics.com; 4, Kathrin Ayer; 4–5, ©Doug Perrine/Nature Picture Library; 6, ©Doug Perrine/Nature Picture Library; 7BKG, ©Doug Perrine/Nature Picture Library; 8 (inset), ©Frans Lanting/Minden Pictures; 8–9, ©SA TEAM/Foto Natura/Minden Pictures; 10, ©Doug Perrine/Seapics.com; 11, ©Valerie Taylor/Ardea.com; 12, ©Frans Lanting/Minden Pictures; 13, ©Peter Oxford/Nature Picture Library; 14 (inset), ©Steve Winter/National Geographic/Getty Images; 14–15, ©Masahiro Iijima/Ardea.com; 16 (inset), ©Jean Lecomte/BIOS/Peter Arnold; 16–17, ©Peggy Stop/Seapics.com; 18–19, ©John Swedborg/Ardea.com; 20–21, ©Frans Lanting/Minden Pictures; 22L, ©Peter Oxford/Nature Picture Library; 22C, ©François Gohier/Ardea.com; 22R, ©C.C. Lockwood/Bruce Coleman; 23TL, ©Doug Perrine/Nature Picture Library; 23TR, ©William H. Ames/Bruce Coleman; 23BL, ©Olivier Grunewald/Oxford Scientific; 23BR, ©Solvin Zankl/Nature Picture Library; 23BKG, ©M. Watson/Ardea.com.

Publisher: Kenn Goin
Senior Editor: Lisa Wiseman
Editorial Development: Nancy Hall, Inc.
Creative Director: Spencer Brinker
Photo Researcher: Carousel Research, Inc.: Mary Teresa Giancoli
Design: Otto Carbajal

Library of Congress Cataloging-in-Publication Data

Hall, Kirsten.
    Leatherback turtle : the world's heaviest reptile / by Kirsten Hall.
        p. cm.—(SuperSized!)
Includes bibliographical references and index.
ISBN-13: 978-1-59716-393-4 (library binding)
ISBN-10: 1-59716-393-7 (library binding)
1. Leatherback turtle—Juvenile literature. I. Title.

QL666.C546H35 2007
597.92'89—dc22

                    2006033247

For more information, write to Bearport Publishing Company, Inc., 101 Fifth Avenue, Suite 6R, New York, New York 10003. Printed in the United States of America.

10 9 8 7 6 5 4 3 2 1

Contents

One Heavy Turtle

The leatherback turtle is the heaviest reptile in the world.

A leatherback turtle weighs about as much as a male Atlantic walrus.

A leatherback turtle can weigh
up to 2,000 pounds (907 kg).
It can grow up to 9 feet
(3 m) long.

Ocean Divers

Leatherback turtles live in oceans all around the world.

They spend most of their time underwater.

These big turtles are good divers.

They can dive deeper than any other reptile.

A leatherback turtle can dive more than 3,900 feet (1,189 m). The deepest a scuba diver has gone is 1,027 feet (313 m).

Leatherback Turtles in the Wild

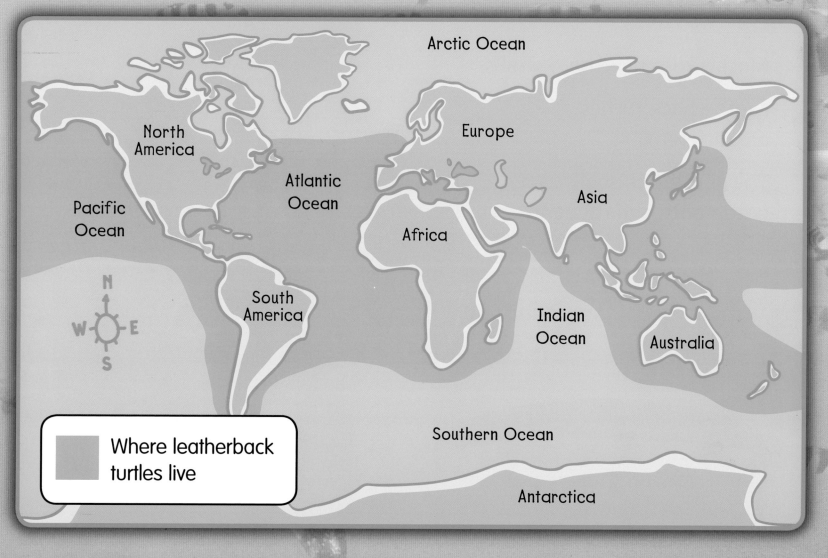

Arctic Ocean

North America

Europe

Atlantic Ocean

Asia

Pacific Ocean

Africa

N
W E
S

South America

Indian Ocean

Australia

Where leatherback turtles live

Southern Ocean

Antarctica

A Thin Shell

Most turtles have hard **shells**.

Leatherback turtles are different.

They have thin shells that are smooth and rubbery.

shell

A leatherback turtle's shell can bend slightly.

8

Flippers for Swimming

A leatherback turtle has four **flippers**.

The two front ones push the turtle through water.

The two smaller back flippers help the turtle turn in different directions.

front flippers

A leatherback's front flippers can be almost 9 feet (3 m) across from the tip of one flipper to the tip of the other.

Digging Nests

Leatherback turtles hatch from eggs.

At night female leatherbacks crawl onto beaches.

They dig nests and lay their eggs in them.

After they cover the nests with sand, they go back to the ocean.

A female leatherback lays about 80 eggs at a time.

eggs

Baby Steps

After about 60 days, the baby turtles hatch.

They dig their way out from underneath the sand.

Then the little turtles crawl quickly to the ocean.

Baby leatherback turtles are called **hatchlings**.

hatchling

A Belly Full of Jelly

Baby and adult leatherbacks eat mostly **jellyfish**.

They also eat other sea animals that have soft bodies.

A leatherback turtle's jaws cut food like a pair of scissors.

jellyfish

Trouble for Turtles

People can harm leatherback turtles.

The big turtles often get caught in fishing nets and drown.

Plastic bags and other garbage are thrown into the ocean.

The turtles sometimes eat them by mistake and die.

Some people steal leatherback eggs from nests. Then they sell the eggs as food.

Helping Leatherbacks

Leatherbacks have been around for millions of years.

Today, they are in danger.

Many countries now have laws to protect leatherbacks.

These laws help keep these big turtles safe.

A leatherback turtle can live to be 50 years old.

More Heavy Turtles

Leatherback turtles belong to a group of animals called reptiles. Most reptiles hatch from eggs. Except for the leatherback turtle, all reptiles are cold-blooded. Turtles are the only reptiles with shells.

Here are three more heavy turtles.

Galapagos Giant Tortoise

The Galapagos giant tortoise is a turtle that lives on land. It can weigh up to 600 pounds (272 kg).

Loggerhead Turtle

The loggerhead turtle can weigh up to 350 pounds (159 kg).

Alligator Snapping Turtle

The alligator snapping turtle can weigh up to 250 pounds (113 kg).

Leatherback Turtle:
2,000 pounds/907 kg

Galapagos Giant Tortoise:
600 pounds/272 kg

Loggerhead Turtle:
350 pounds/159 kg

Alligator Snapping Turtle:
250 pounds/113 kg

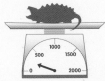

Glossary

flippers (FLIP-urz) broad limbs that help sea animals to swim

jellyfish (JEL-ee-*fish*) an animal that lives in the ocean and has a soft body and long tentacles

hatchlings (HACH-lingz) animals that have recently come out of eggs

shells (SHELZ) the outer coverings of certain animals, such as turtles

Index

Read More

Hickman, Pamela. *Turtle Rescue: Changing the Future for Endangered Wildlife.* Ontario, Canada: Firefly Books (2005).

Rhodes, Mary Jo, and David Hall. *Sea Turtles.* Danbury, CT: Children's Press (2005).

Watt, Melanie E. *Leatherback Turtles.* Milwaukee, WI: Raintree Publishers (2001).

Learn More Online

To learn more about leatherback turtles, visit **www.bearportpublishing.com/SuperSized**